STRANGE WORLD

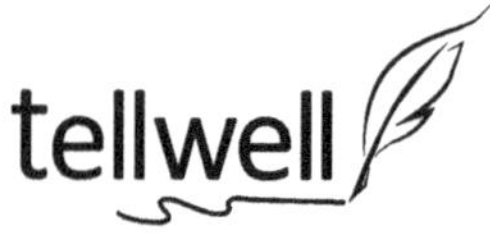

Tellwell Talent

www.tellwell.ca

ISBN

978-1-77370-540-8 (Paperback)

A

journey

through

the breath

of life.

STRANGE WORLD

Nathaniel Brydges

CHAPTER 1:

Flying Free

Flying freely soaring along silver lines

Along the sky's streams breeze reflection

Contorting among the rivers rise.

The alluring sum of glittering shine of the waters surface
that I'm not bound by.

I prow the sky.

What a profound life, to live above the grounds height.

Love of the sounds of the whispers when I glide.

Nothing hinders my strides.

But there is a something that must be rendered in my life.

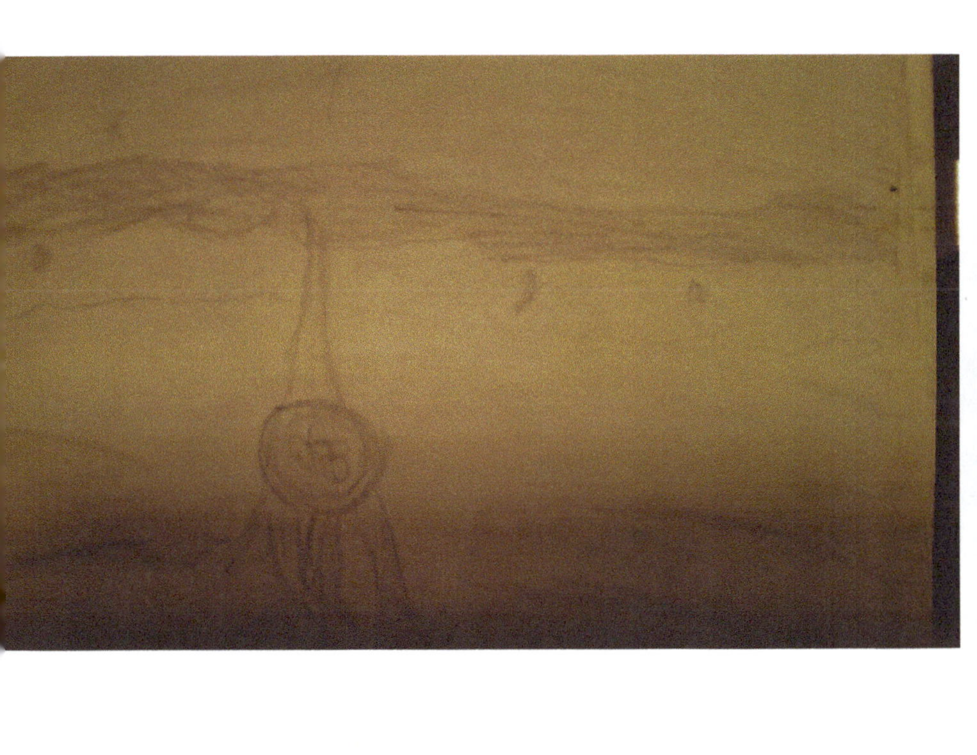

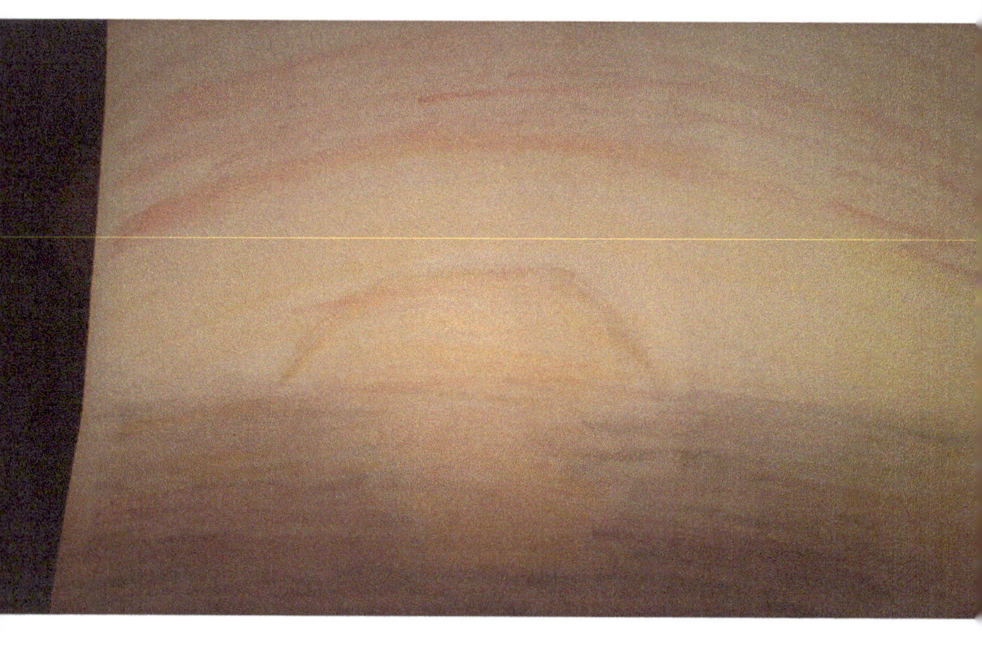

But there is a something that must be rendered in my life

The lives that will live beyond my understanding.

Though it is me that binds the apples of my eye.

They must live on with their own hungers and standing.

It is under mandate that these children must see more to life
    than I can provide

You must make your own home.

And life roam and stride to go

Fly free as me in the sky with all your pride.

Live beyond my life with no strife.

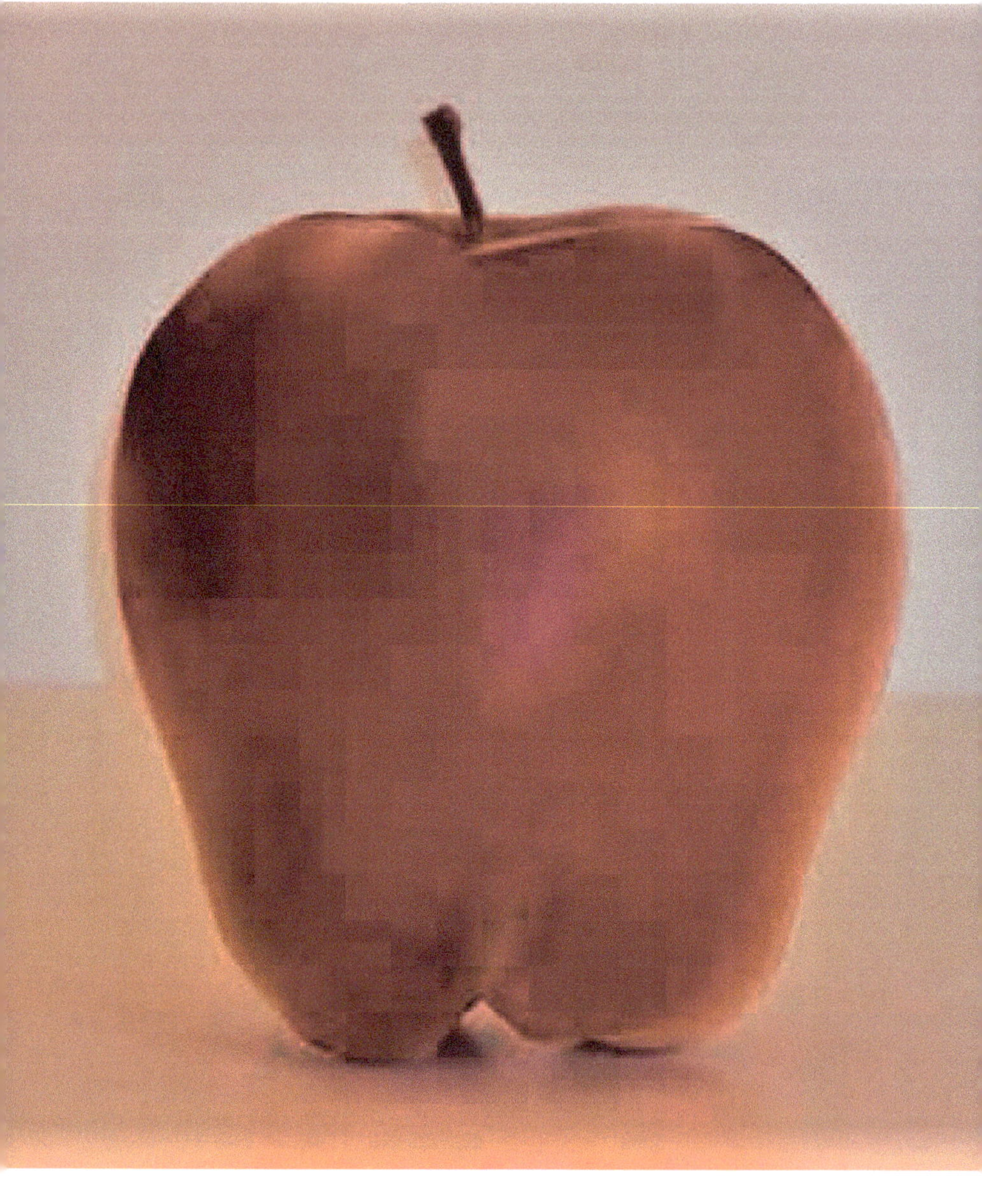

CHAPTER 2
Changing Tides

See the sea, as a ghost rising beyond the Trees!

Basked by the glow of the havens that can be

seen, though the vast scene, simply moves well pass me,
and I a mere man will never know the true depth of all
it's majesty.

And yet the singes of a small it's past lives

It can be preserved with my eyes, as it augments this

Odd mist, mere distortions of a small time.

The colors, a peace beyond bliss, are the only way I

can describe.

And yet the sea in the sky.

Needs to fall, as if the beauty of void demands the blue eye
    to cry.

And it lies as a mass at my feet, like a glass sheet.

It holds a small secret, which I couldn't even hope to grasp
    in my dreams.

So my knowledge can only be called half fantasies.

Needing improvement, and study, while the heavens will
    keep moving pass me.

As the mist is compelled into place,

And held into shape.

It is propelled back to the earth from whence it came.

A form of self driving solely by wait.

To engage in an onslaught agents aged lava.

The illusion is that this is a braided dogma.

But in truth when the elements engage in a hor-
    monal mantra.

It creates the primordial malt to slurp.

To make the high soil, which we engage our lives on.

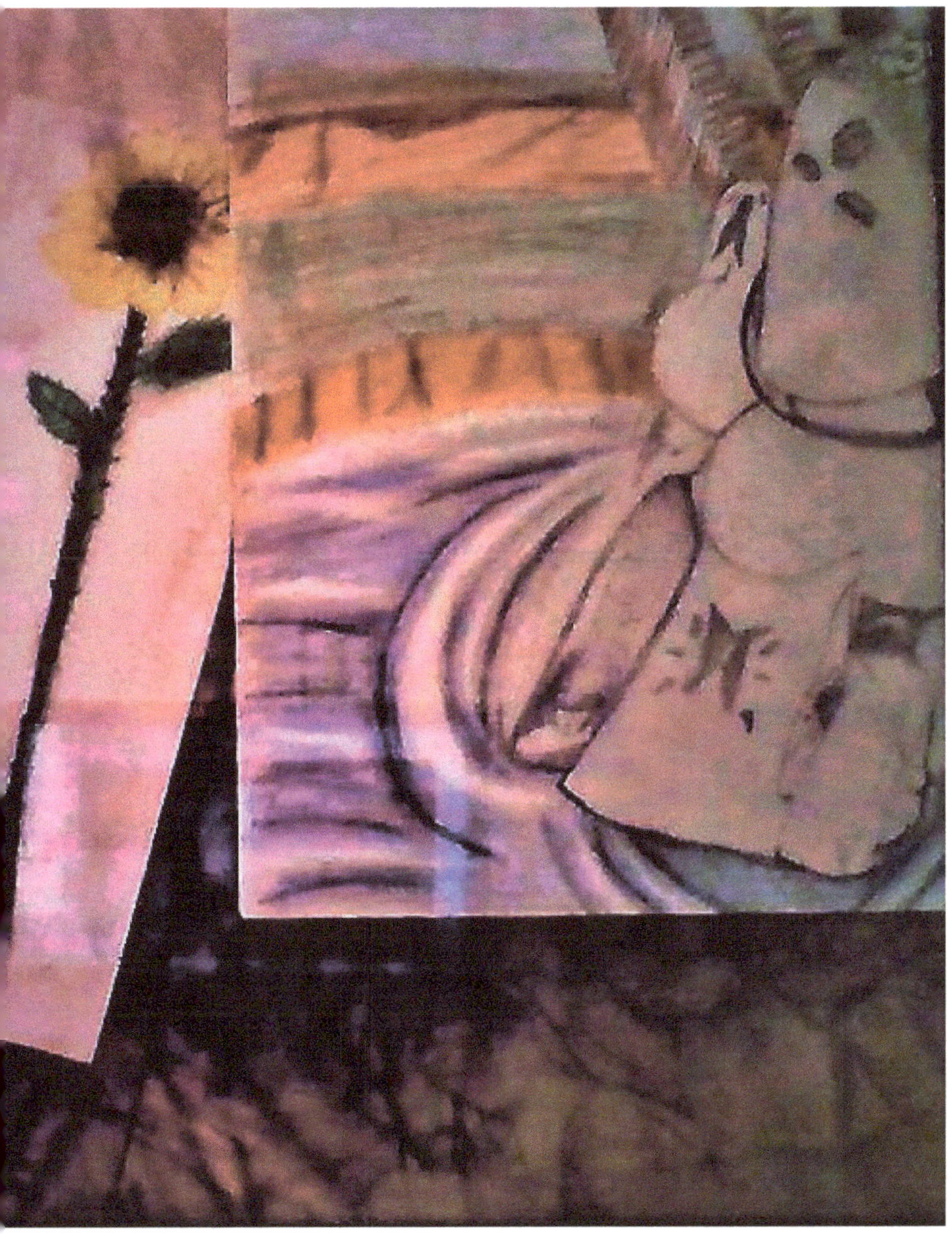

Through out the millennia we've had many mythologies that
   have begetting us.

Though not all were aloud this gift of the alms with proclivi-
   ties forced on curtain individuals.

To which has instilled harm on to the seeds of those called
   different, as the reciprocals.

This repelled qualms;

Violent storms instead of the health of harmony.

An almost endless flow.

Time repeating, in different lives upon the old's completion.

Just like tides receding.

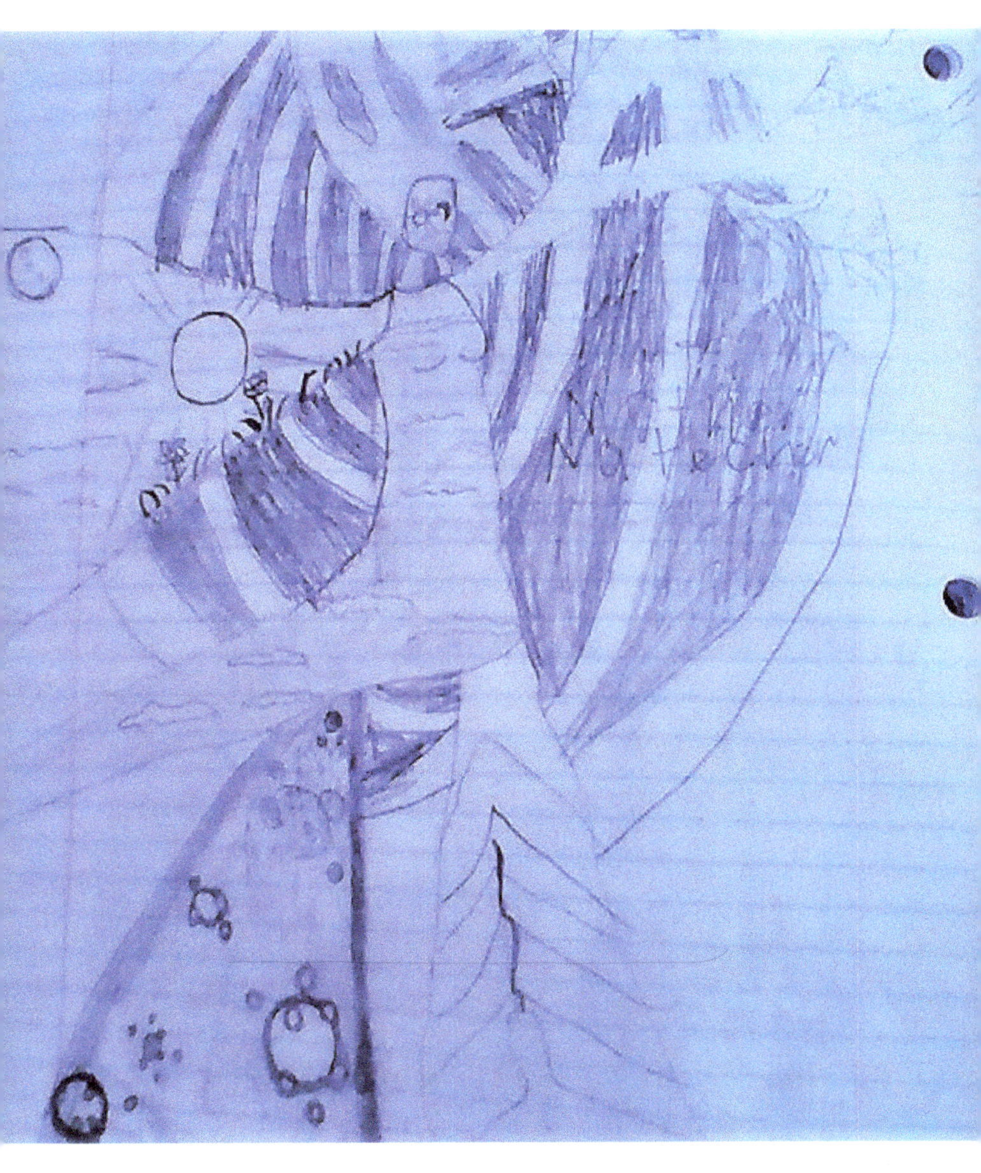

Nightwalker

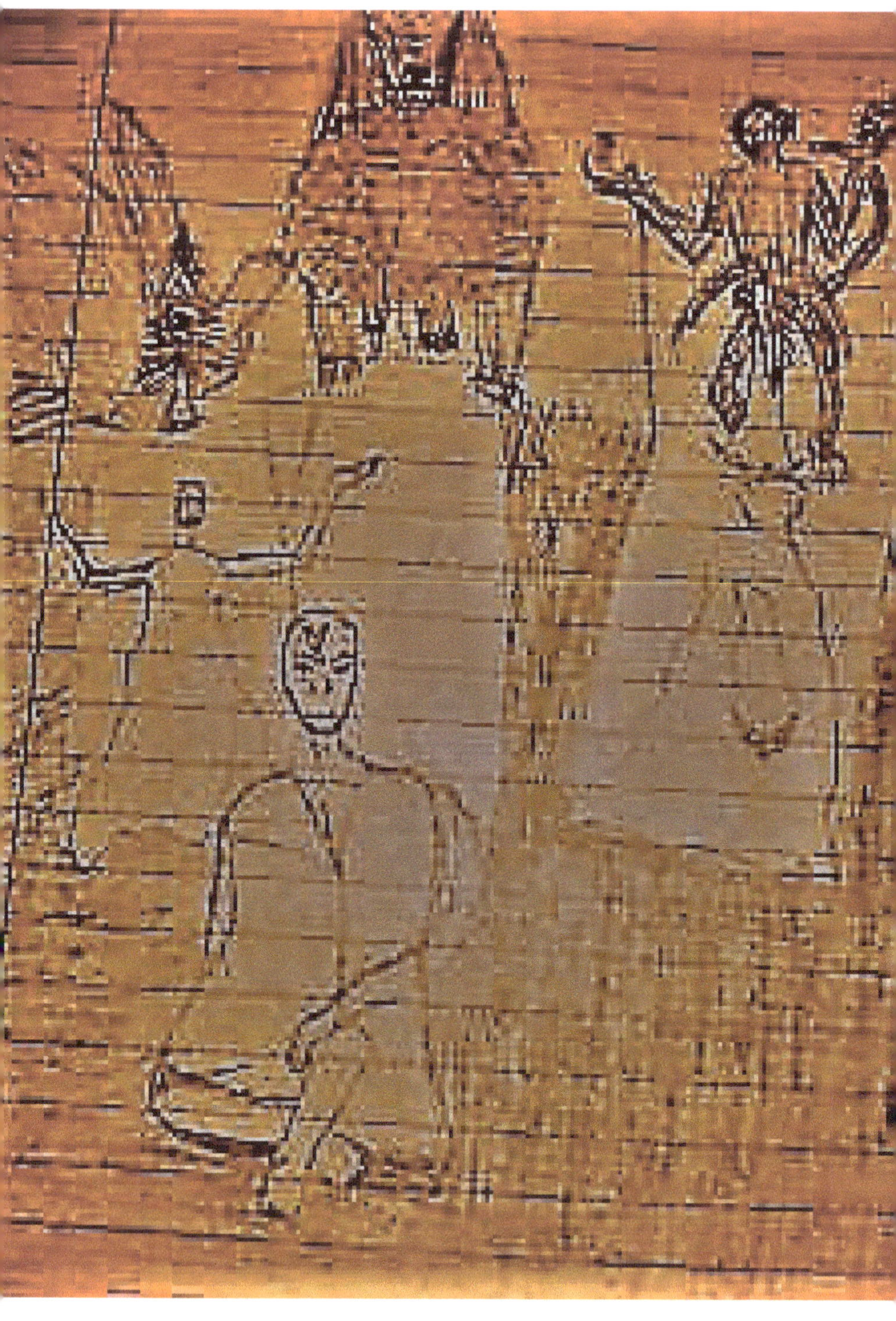

But what if we could more beyond it.

What if all stories were created equal.

And all people were allowed to add upon myth.

What if all thoughts, feelings, and sensation, were to find
    a place to congregate at.

A place where we embrace all leagues of intuition.

No matter the faces, races, creed's or religions.

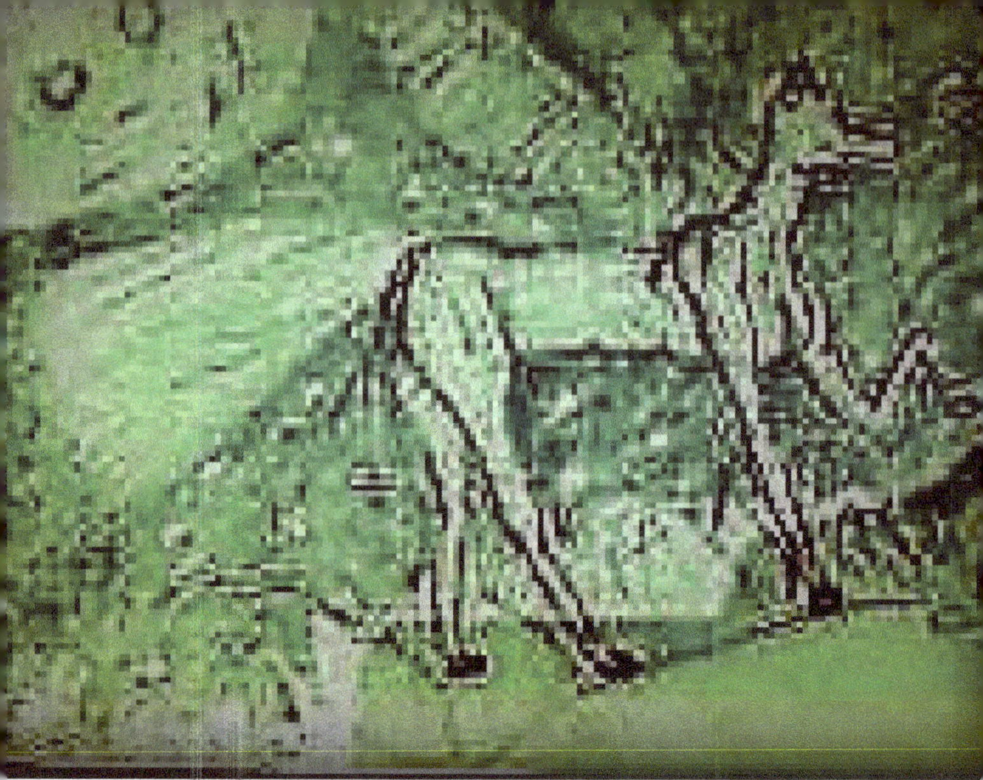

A new story, where all thoughts can be reborn.

Without hate or scorn.

Taking a shape, to be adored.

Passions, reactions, and interactions solidified to
   new matters.

Burning, turning, and earning intensified new chapters.

I would love to see the limits of the human mind. Through
   out all walks of life.

Endless possibilities with a life as long as time.

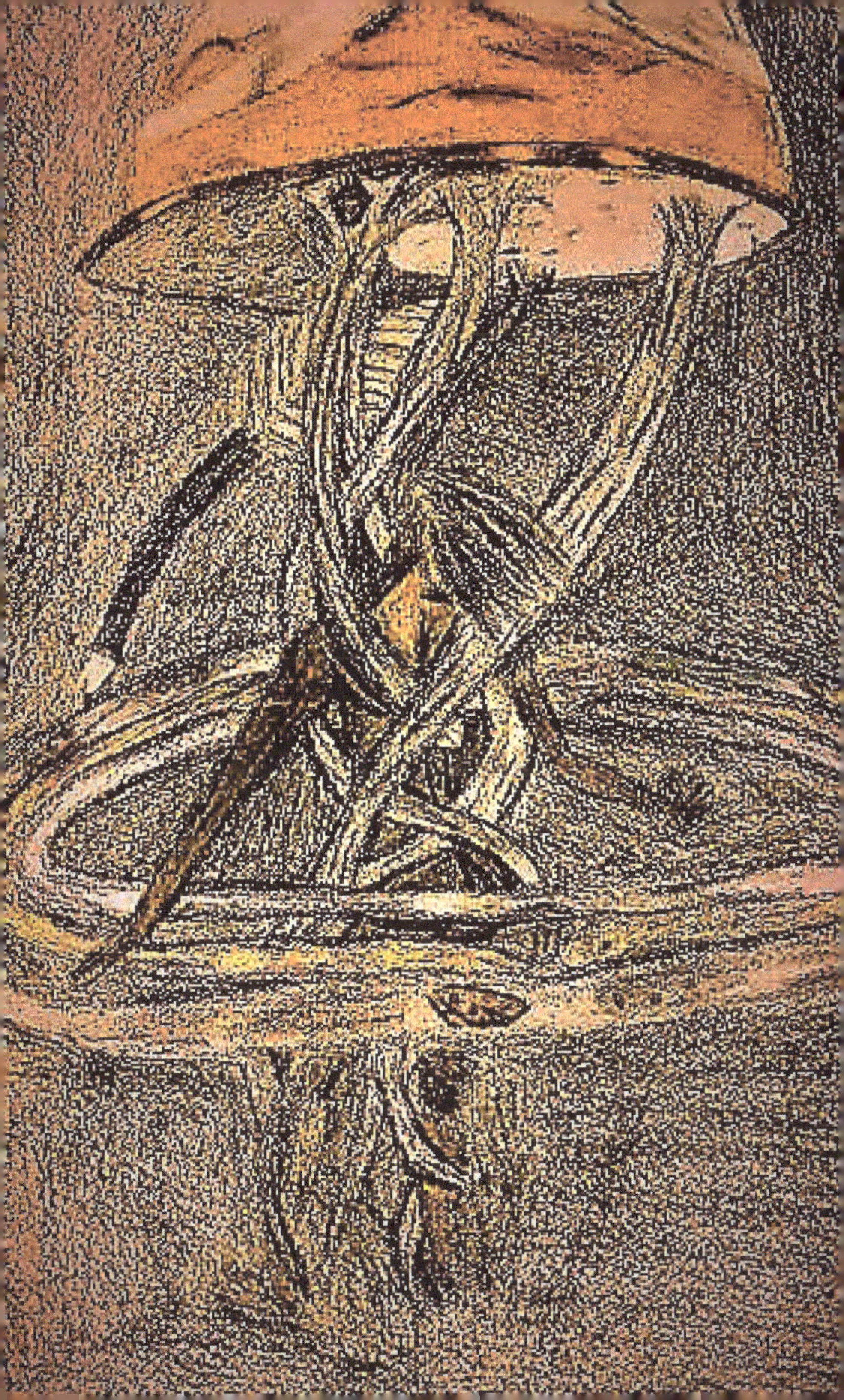

My dream is to make a website where people can create

Their own dream worlds.

Where they can turn their own emotions into other

people, elements, or beasts with their own thoughts
   and morals.

My thoughts are like a multi colored storm; each feeling is
   a bolt of lightning, who's color and shape ever changing!!

And when they pass, it leaves a scar in the clouds with
   a touch of grayness.

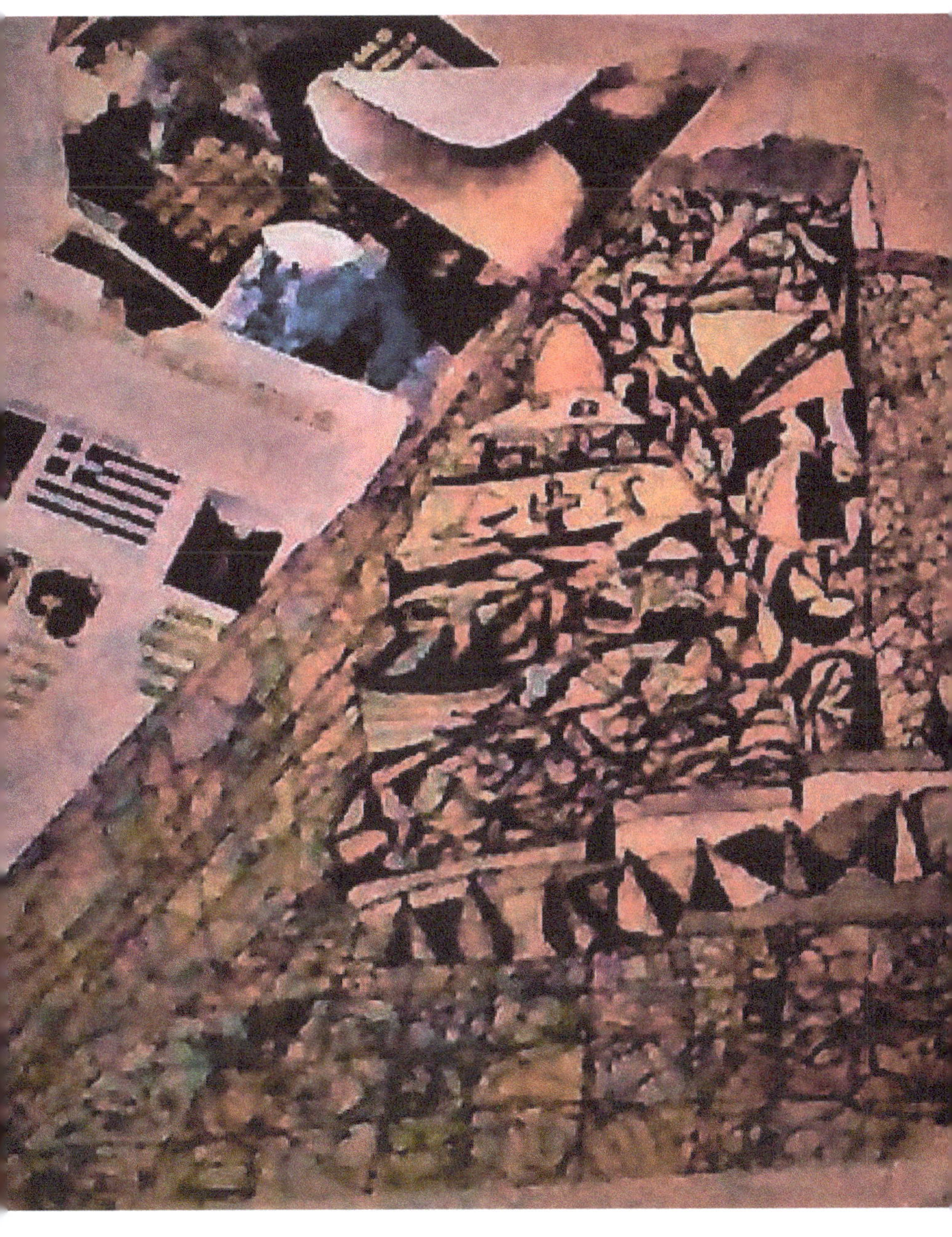

Now I want to know everybody's.

What is the world's dream, and how is it changing?

What is the person next to me thinking?

What shape does it peek in?

Is it water seeping, with a green mist?

Is their anger a caveman painting?

Their happiness trees growing shameless?

Their sadness a flash flood going through the pavement?

What can you see, hear, feel, smell, and tasting?

Is there a sea pear, with eels and shells at the base's end?

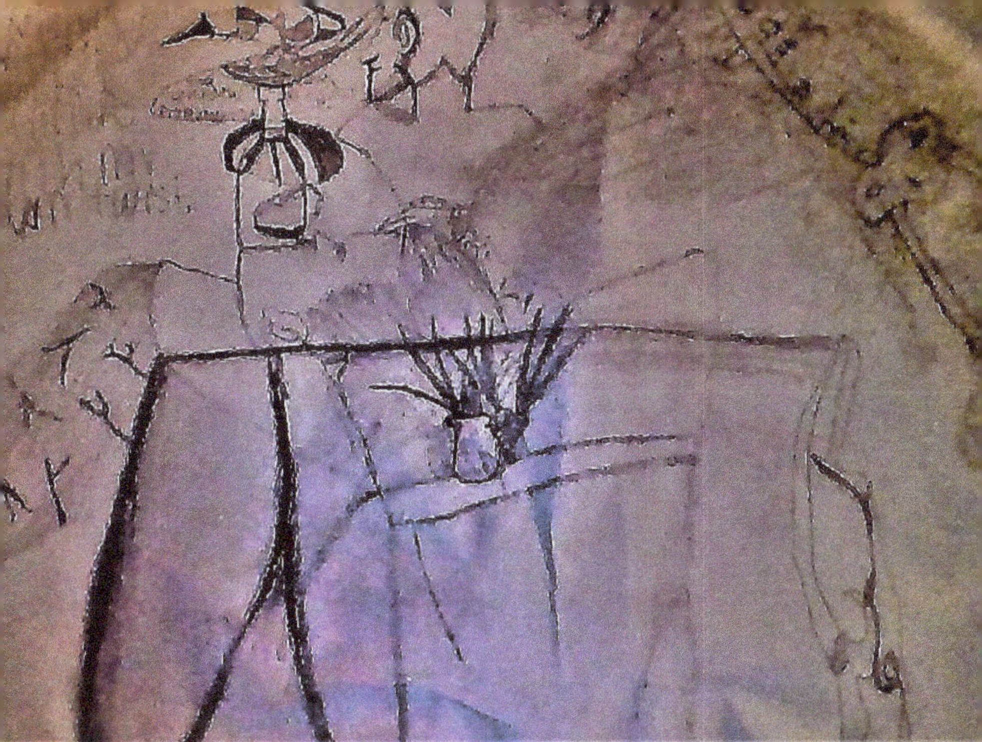

If I see you seeing me, is it like to fun-house mirrors?

Reflecting different visions for all of eternity?

But this only one person, what happens in a crowd?

Is it like the distortion of the telephone game, during a rock consort so loud?

What happens if the same innovative being can happen in a world of dreams?

Is there an end to the possibilities?

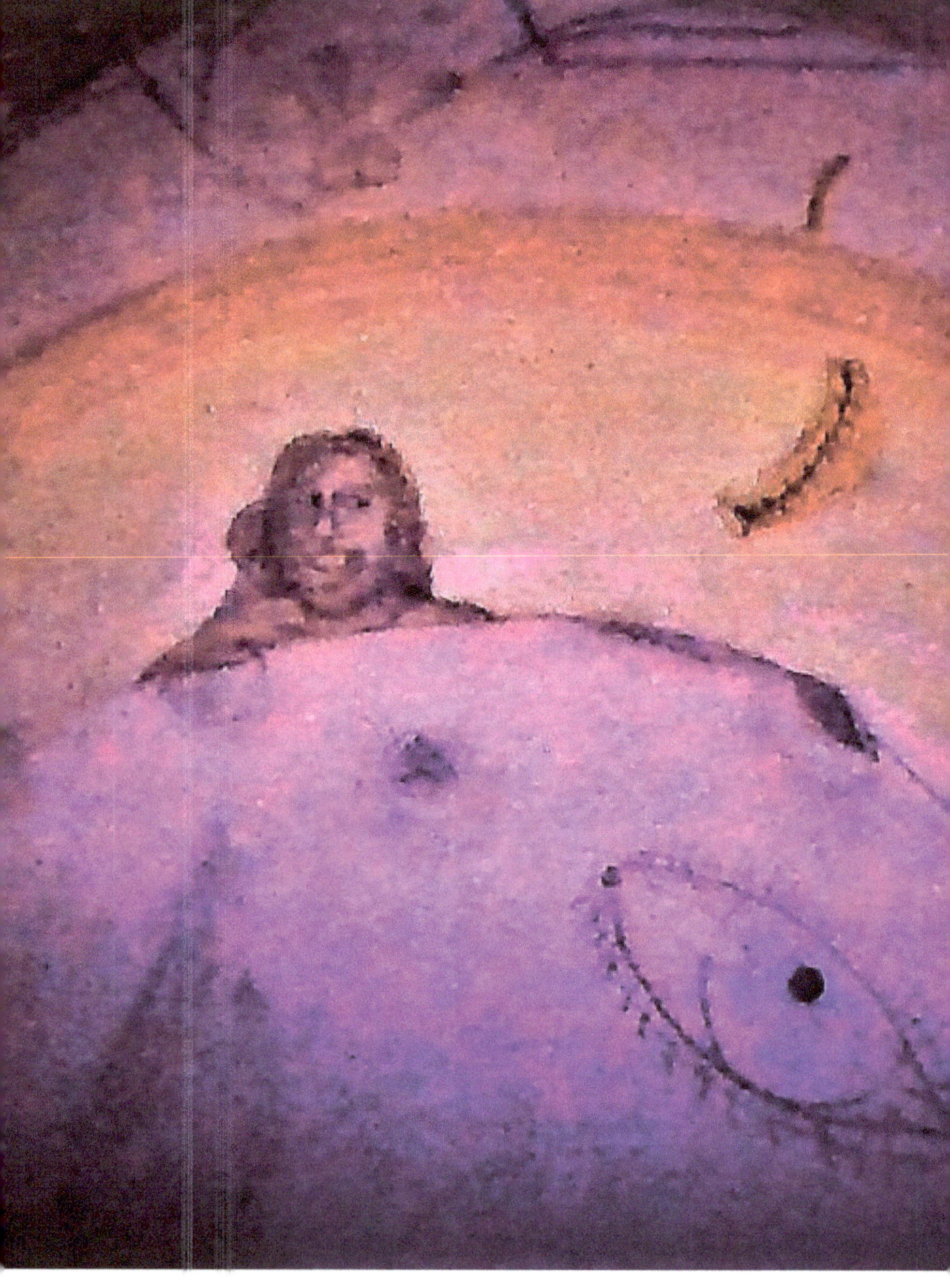

What of the creators that live in all corners?

From the top of the sky, to the base boards in the halls
and forays.

Blue waters, both salty, and fresh.

Nothing truly dies, merely passed on to other lives;

Letting them change our flesh.

So many different perspectives.

And evolution can only happen if we learn from all
others lesions.

How do you perceive your world that is

different from mine?

Different motives? Oracles? Indifference, or passion-
    ate strides?

So many lives, crossing the eroding soulful fields that
    is time.

If we are all new snowflakes

Then I will make a place where can we can all share

The full mystic of the whole of our grace.

I want to see perfect fantasy.

That is how I define my knowledge of reality.

It's not so strange when you think of how we make up
    governments, and words.

Only to corrupted them into profanities.

That's the natural curses of people abiding

to one person's thoughts as absolute.

The reflective can only experience vanity.

Which can lead to calamity.

But I've had a different vision for the future,

where all minds can be seen for all of their majesty.

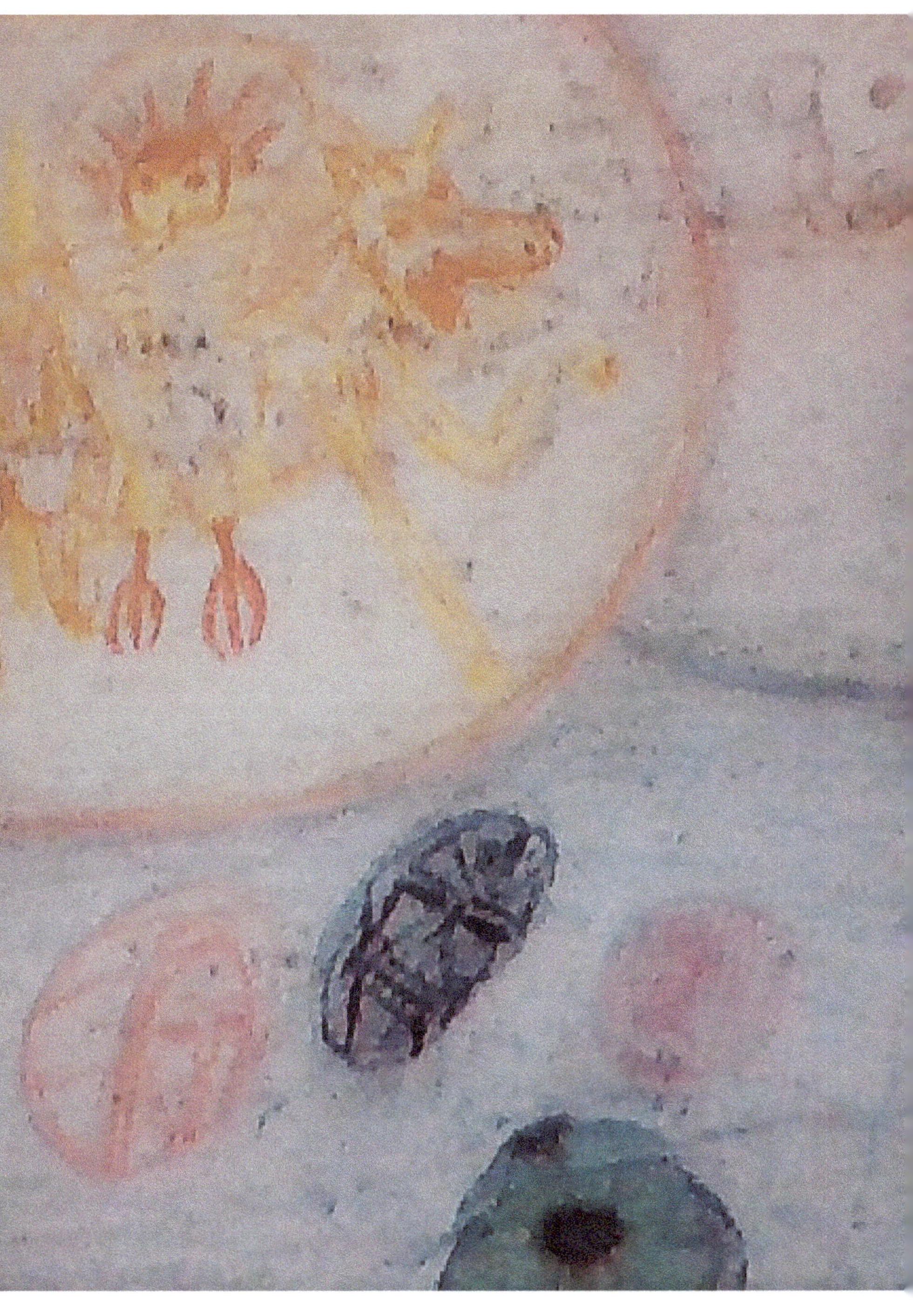

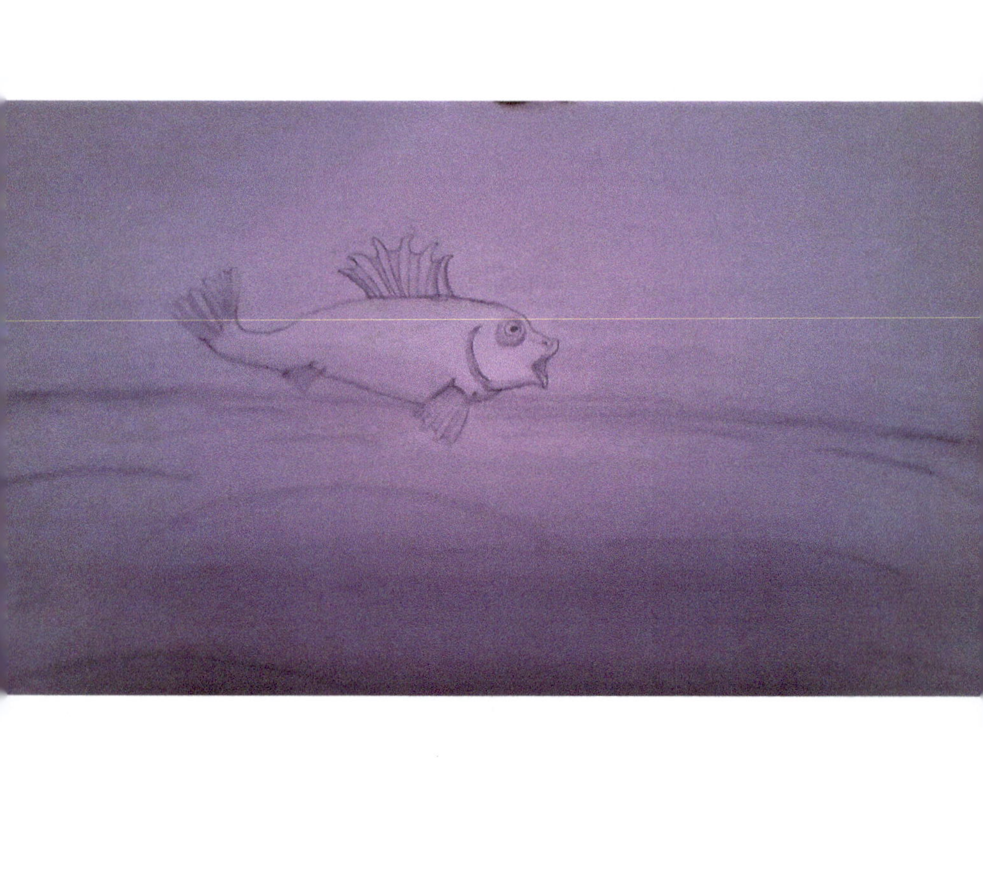

CHAPTER 3

In The Dark

Floating below the surface where the colors are
Impermanent through the surfs mist

So much beauty brought to me to interpret

So many mysteries with inverted wit untouchable no matter
where my assertions hit

How can I know this vast expanse?

Maybe as a ghost a being amassed?

Outside of times vex and cast?

but to me, my life is precious, I need it to progress on.

Maybe that's why?...

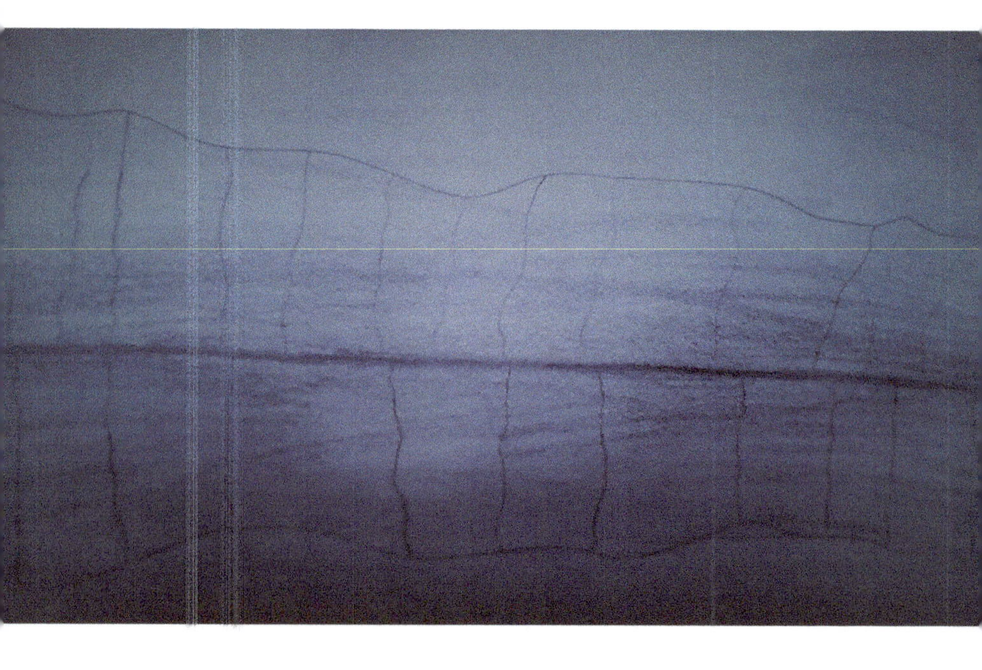

I avoid the abysmal void.

At a centennial point.

It is intentional that I stay critical subjugated, and anoint,
above this dismal joint.

A shadow so pure that even light can't adjoin.

An abyss of lacquer spanning to infinity.

My mind seems to appoint a malice that's an exact thirst
expanding its intensity

A miss the boundless stature standing intensively, at this
mastered fear fanning;

A concept into living with me

Maybe that's why...?

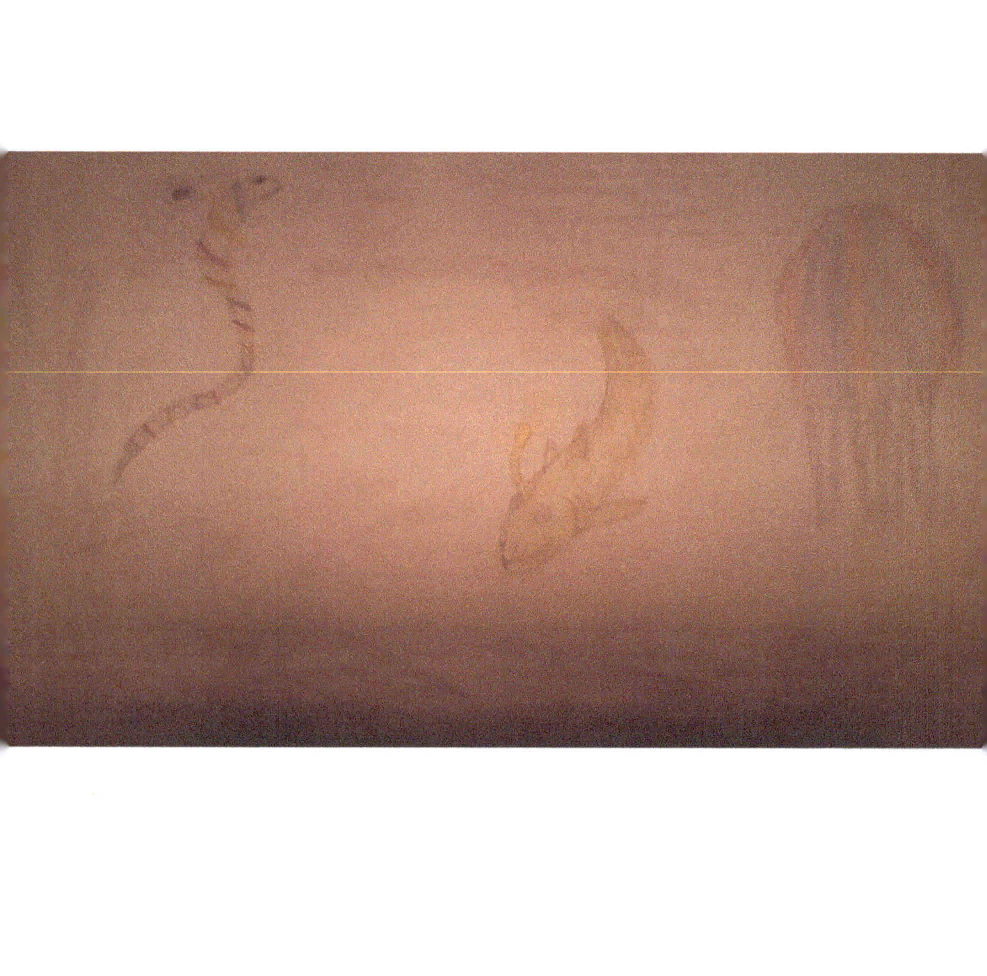

I allowed my direction to pass by the surface being lost
    to me

Like in a past life; my wonderment leading me to move
    through secrets classified.

astonishment feeding spree my mind designed to unleash it.

My imagination wonders satisfied beyond the grasp of what
    I'm faced with.

Hundreds of images that my mind creates.

In intent's feeling like eons of vast expansions.

I move through the enormous darkness.

So still and thick, like a woven carpet.

 I can't even feel my movements or the waters parting.

But I felt that if I kept going;

There would be illumination to engorge this garden.

As I went through the glum I'm faced with there was light in
    the gorge uninhibited with no pardon.

Free in nonrestrictive harmony, I've never seen something so
    beautiful moving so timid, a part of ease.

Such wonders infused and useful with no limit.

I'm glad to be departed from my routine.

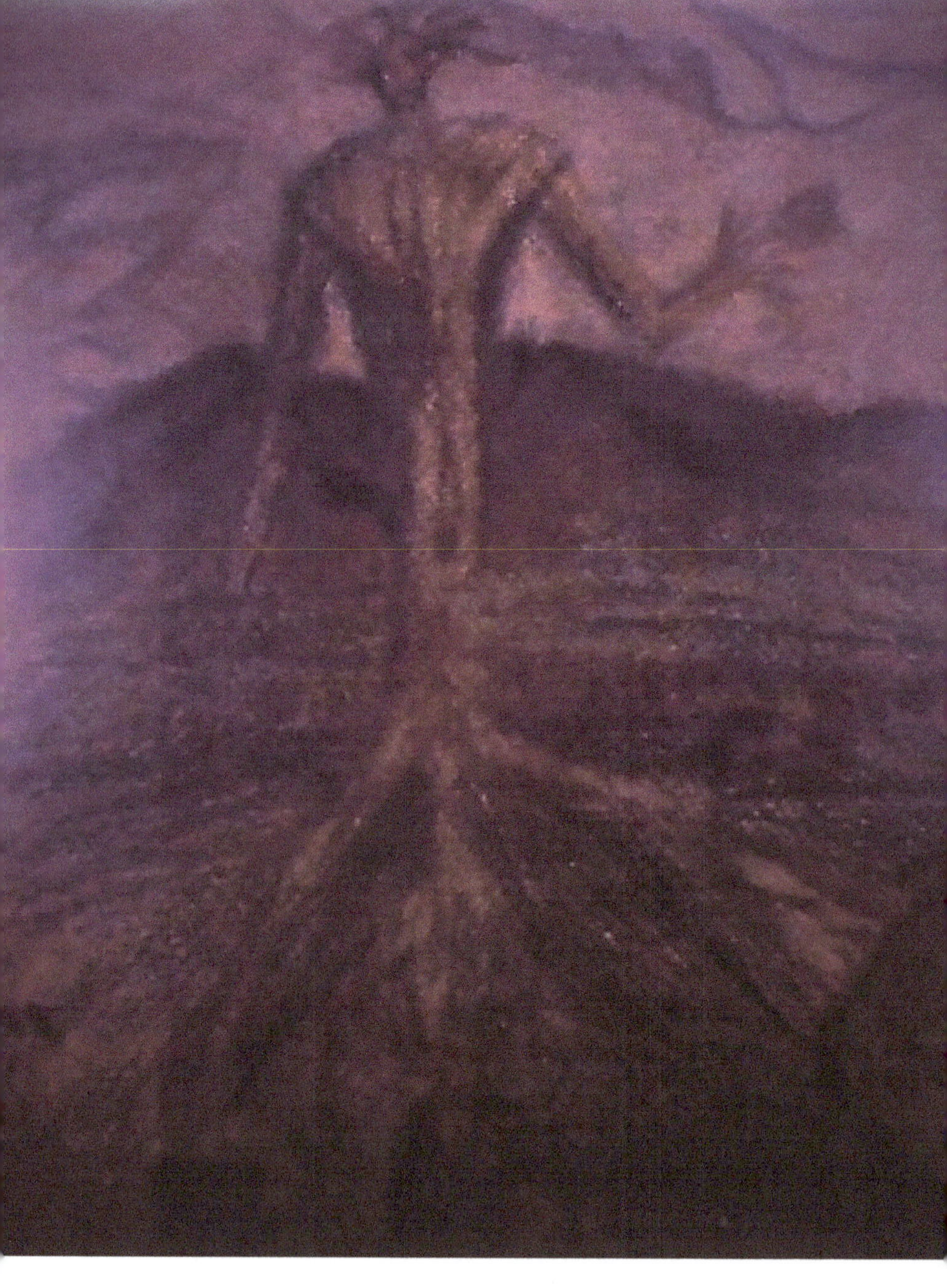

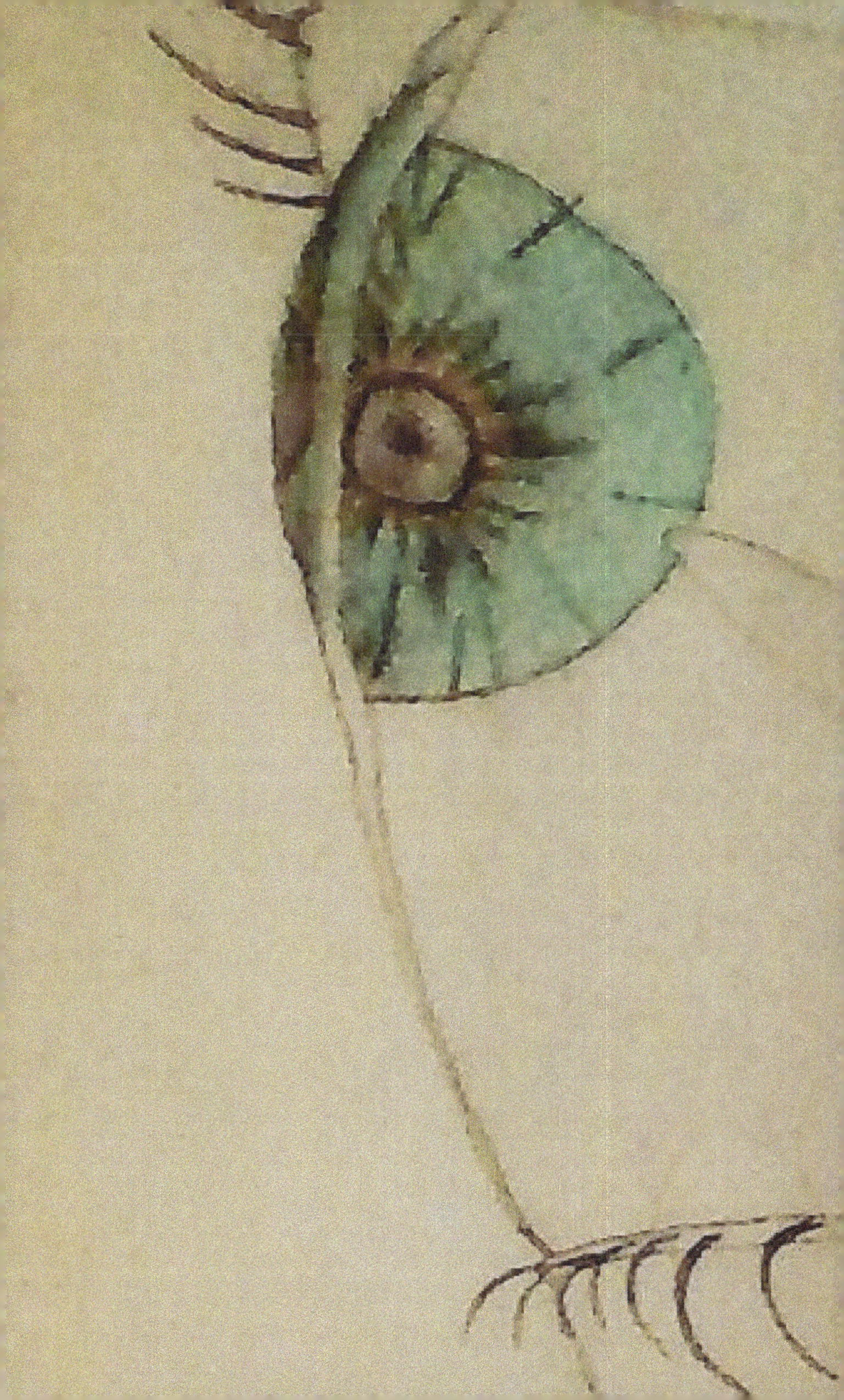

CHAPTER 4

Creation

Weathering storms from the ghost of the sauna.

A blanket with feathers that pours, into the nutritious host
that we stand on top of.

When Zeus's hand smashed the clay, that Cronos engraved,
feeding Poseidon's waves.

Traveling through the mouth of the serpent, a living
soup that is churning in the mysteries lurking in the
murk's depths.

The haven's reflections have been captured

The past's great movement has been embedded in the life
forces collections to bring will and soul into it stature.

To be latched here in life's grand space similar to the heart
of the world's pasture.

All warmed in a mull formed, that made a hammer that
became the heart of Thur from part of its core despite the
fires being an omnivore.

A cannibal, taking all of the smallest and fragile from its
need to bound turning into a vacuum. compressing to
a statue with unknown value.

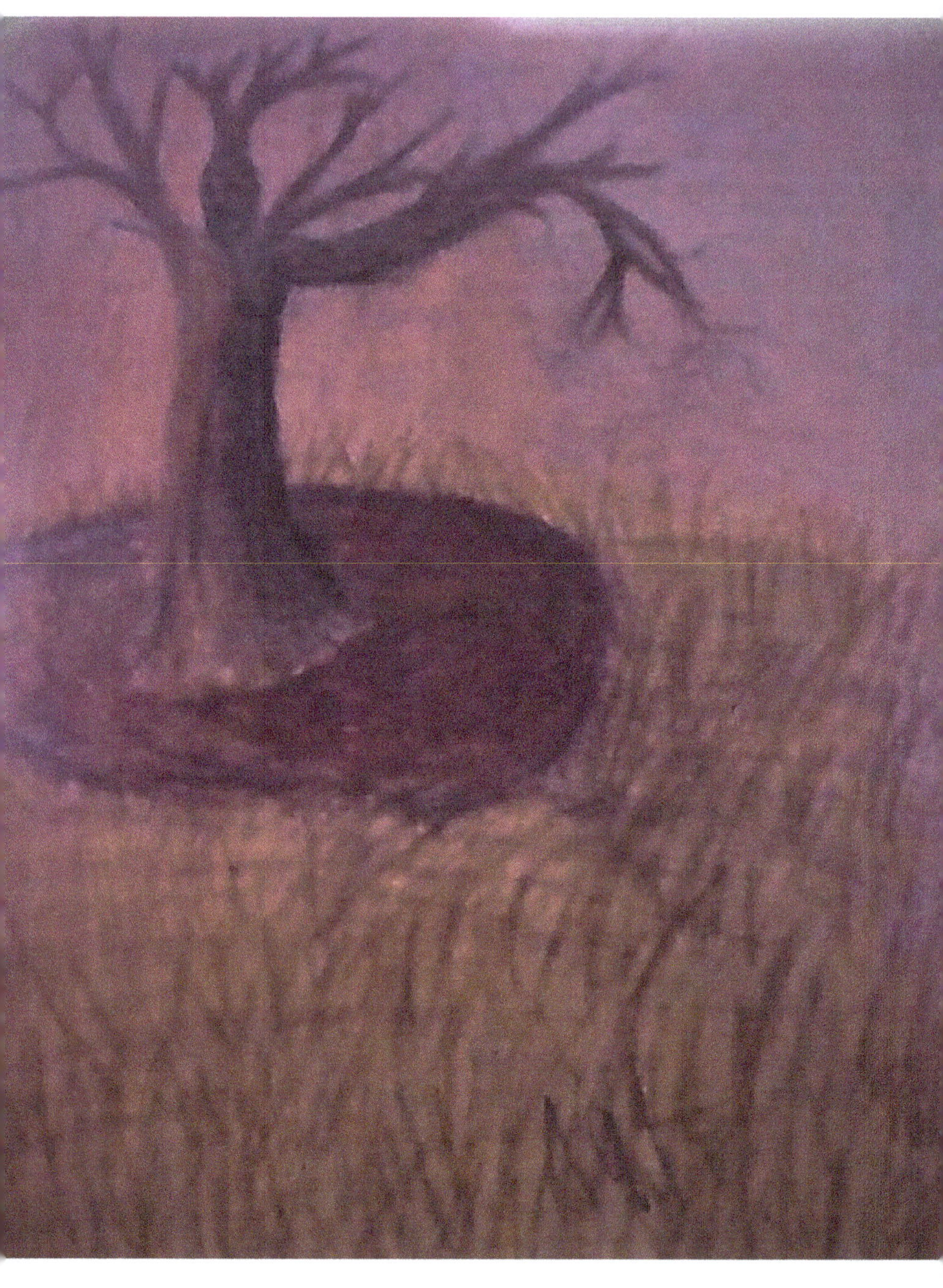

Burning in its end like the mighty Hercules goes it's
introverted needs to the weight of the introverted hurt
and pleas

From the ashes to be dispersed in to what could be inter-
preted as me.

All brought together by the heart of an audience darkness.

Its part of purity from absents ending or starting small
outside and enlarged in.

no malice simply a departing in which even light is torn
apart in the allowance of its scared skin its prowess.

Is greater than times grand-lartsony and fringe escaping all
of father time's imperial is.

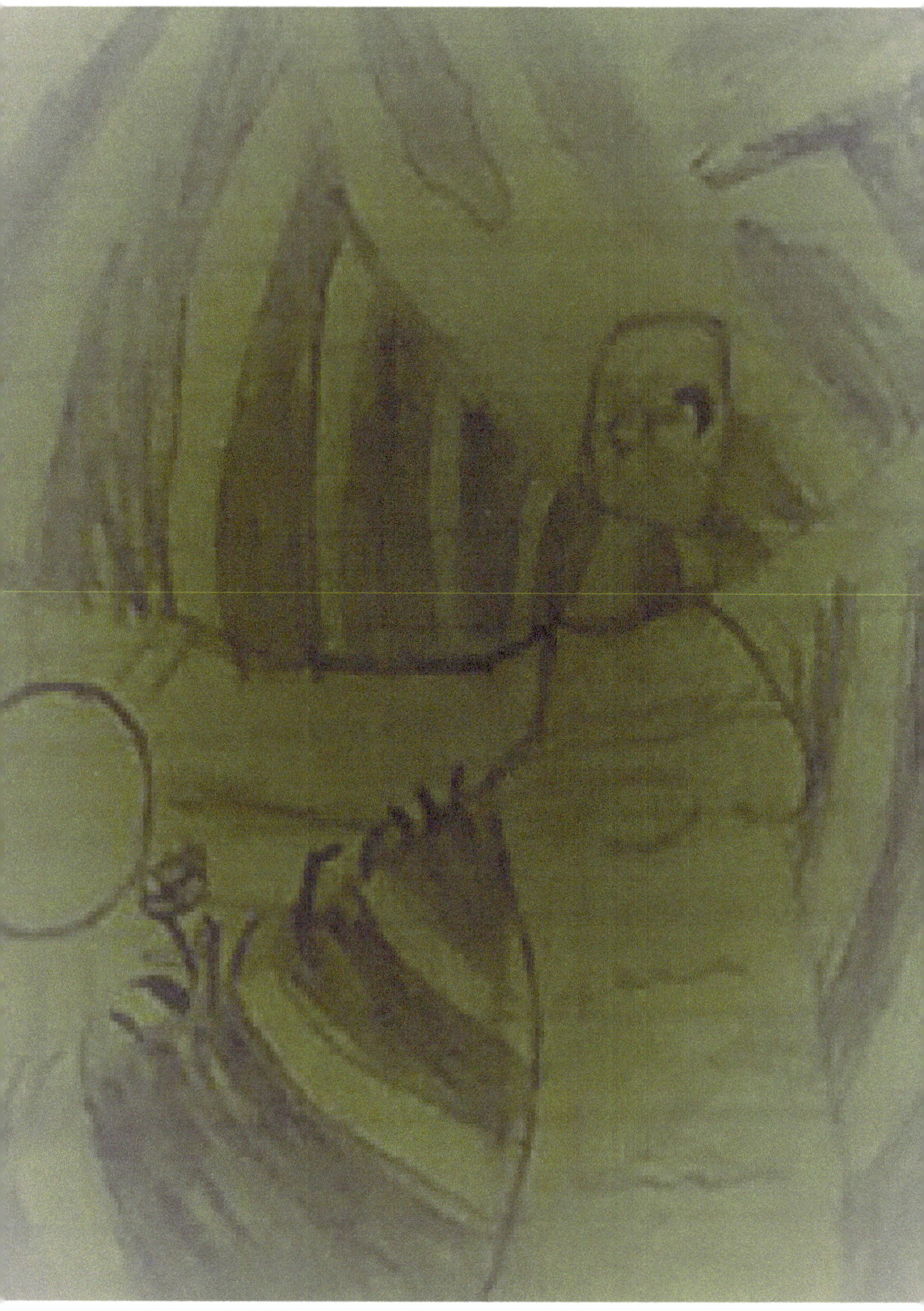

And yet without this darkness light could not be charmed
to exist.

Lightest of all to be farmed into hardness from the ashes of
fire being turned into all gardens;

Lasting beyond all spires and empires for this defines
mother earth

Her power her inspires change from all of her children that
marvel, and emirs from poisonous waters and air, the
lighting imparting a treasure life, rarer than diamonds.

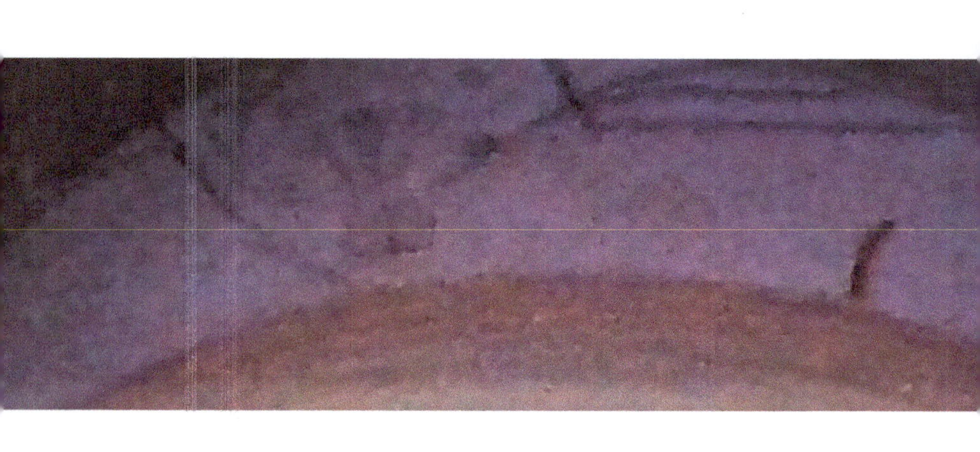

Going back to the beginning of all things when the universe
  was a ball that gleamed, smaller than the head of a pin,
  leaving all angels qualifying.

There were two forces sent to lose their enforcement.

Letting all things loss and poring.

Allowing a perfect reflection to be repute
  through distortions.

What remained was regrouped through absorption, into
  deferent groups flowing through different courses

With various sleuths of course lengths.

Interlude with different times coursing.

Confused with all forces; intoned to create all definitions of
    what is important.

Moon and ocean, ocean and moon.

Forever to loom out of focus yet still devoted and swooned

With such great distance in-between their existence still in
    each-others visions.

Like pictures of love ones who are missing

Carbon and methane dancing with chemistry

Smashing to create electricity, compacted to simplicity,
    interacting with the poisons liquid amenity

Brewing the primal soup that will be tasted with burning the
    poisonous gas to breath

The soup must compacted, into so the hard
    waters compassion.

With the acids intertwined into its own infatuation.

Its jets to stop fasting from the deadly air, burning the greens
    breath to make the vapors from its passion.

all of these intermediate actions given all pulses who was,
    and that is.

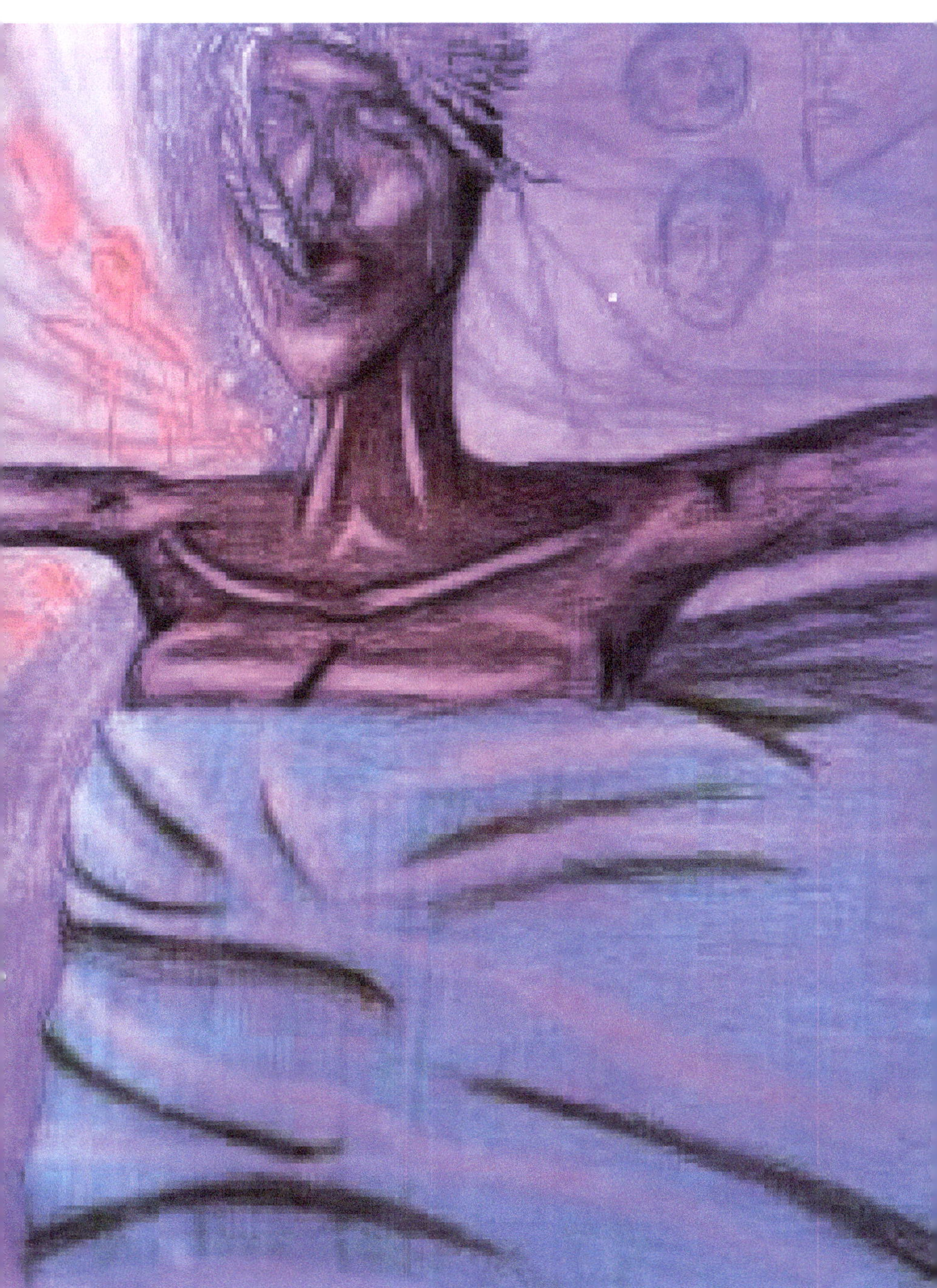

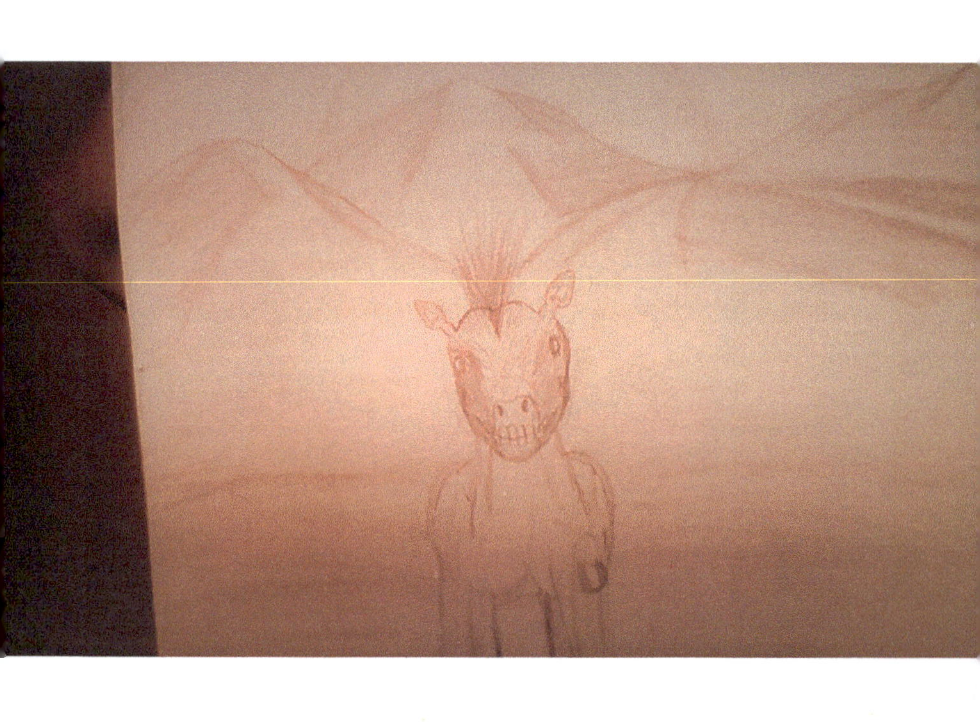

CHAPTER 5
Running

Running, running till my legs are pumping battery acid

Chest like a weight a burning stove.

Feet a consent thumping madly prancing trying to beat.

The closing of the sun's gate.

The alluring.

The grove with the feeling that someday I'll find it, as

long as my feet don't stop turning dirt.

Push through the churning hurt. never looking back, return-
   ing has never been

what I'm worth.

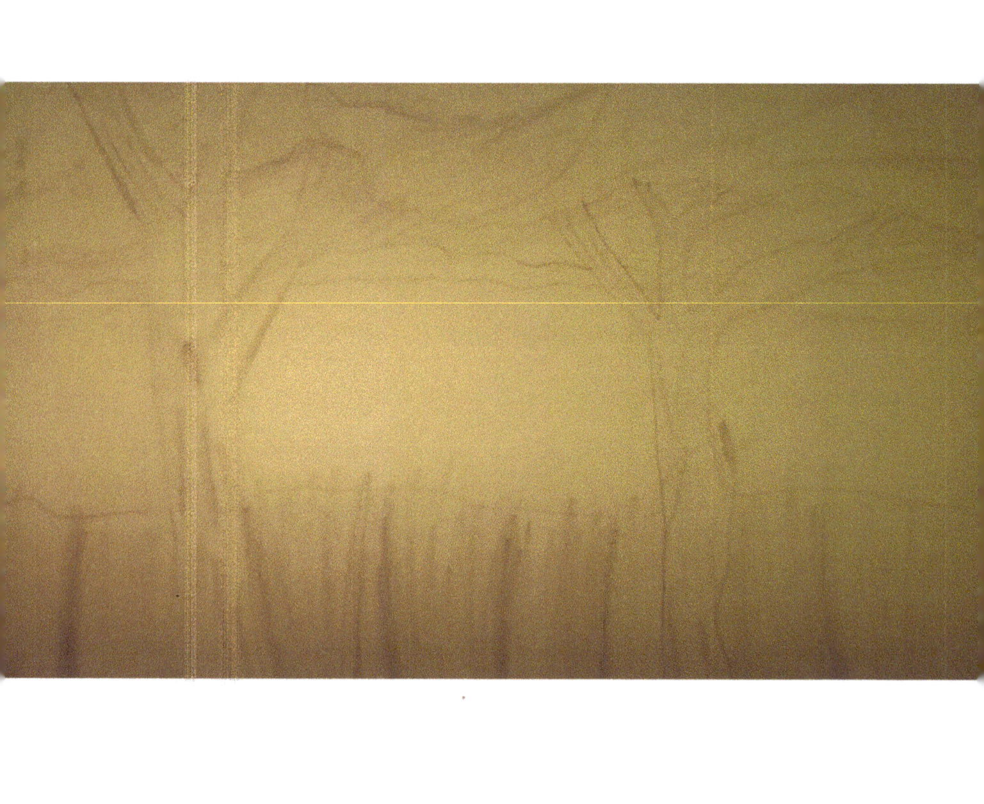

Moving through lushes groves, and bountiful floral brushes
bestowed at mountains full in the soil.

Creatures and insects living beneath the earth where the
seeds rest to feast, and

birth that life enlist.

The endurance of these living things to.

Bare the seasons and flourish in spite of their misgivings
depriving their needs.

ensnared by what destiny, completion or depletion on what
mother nature encourages.

And as they do I must push through to find the jewel as
    it blooms.

There it is, a red ruby it's head shines like jewelry.

 I question if my eyes are lead to be deceived.

The vanes of the wood pumping Raw nutriment.

 So beautiful, no shame could be drawn from the interpreted
    from the lurking gift.

Just off the branch of the swirling cliff so alluring.

By pushing my body past it's limits moving forward never to
    give in.

The fruit of my labors and my dreams, I now have the proof
    displayed here with gleams.

 I stood willing to saver all of the croup's purred into
    a cream.

This taste is my reword for not giving up on being me this
    apple is the principal of myself thinking my dreams
    are indispensable.

We all can move beyond the predictable, if we brake through
    our enlisted stone in each individual;

then we can all reach the end of our goals.

Don't give up!

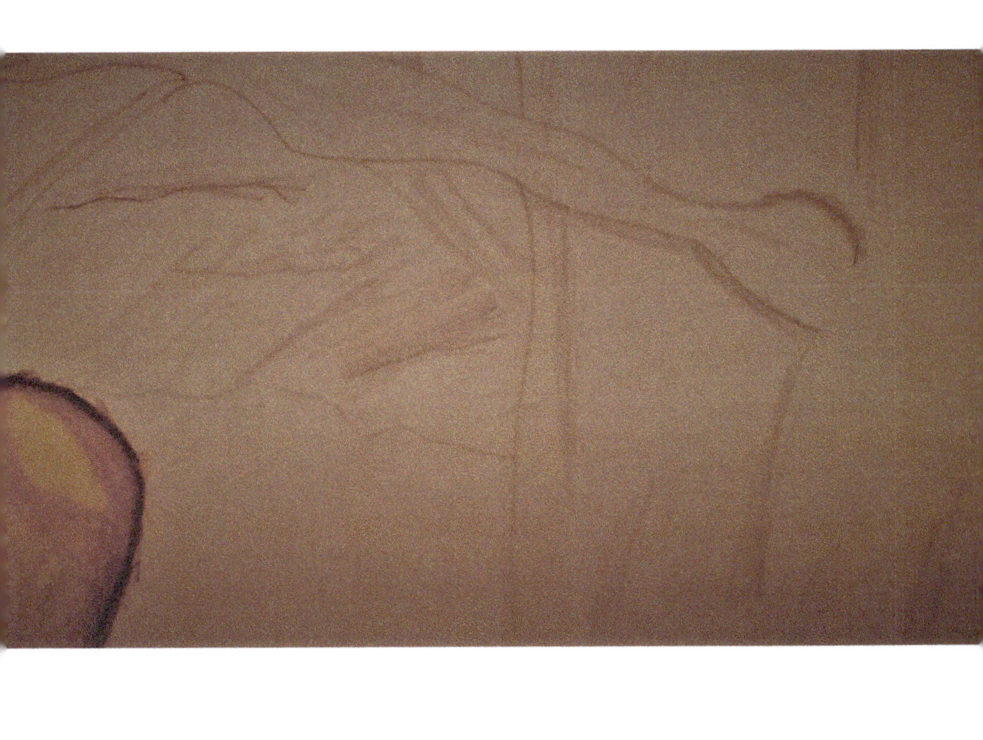